Grandma's Notes on Parenting

Dedicated to my two beautiful and amazing daughters

Melissa and Angela

their husbands Nick and Jon

and my wonderful new grandson, Landon.

I hope that it will inspire parents to love their children

and become a positive role model.

INTRODUCTION

Being a parent is a tough job, a really tough job! No instruction manual comes with a new baby, but who would take time to read it anyway? Besides, how difficult can it be to raise a child? You might think that way until you actually become a parent for the first time.

How do new parents prepare for a baby?

Do we realize how special babies are and what an enormous task it will be to care for a tiny, fragile human life that will soon be placed into our hands?

Are we ready to be totally responsible for the future of another human being?

Do we spend time reading books, watching videos or attending classes?

If you were anything like me or most other parents, you did absolutely nothing except wait for this miracle to happen and assume that you would naturally learn as you go. It's really sad when we look back at our lives and see how unprepared we were to take care of this special new arrival. We spend more time planning a vacation or planting a garden than we do for such an amazing and important life event. Even the baby's room gets more attention than the baby itself. Some people spend hours choosing specific paint colours and wallpaper. Baby furniture and accessories are carefully picked out. When the time gets closer, parties are planned and attended where the parents receive all sorts of unique and colourful baby items.

Then the new arrival comes and confusion starts. Some new parents actually do take pre-natal classes to learn about caring for a new baby. But this only covers basic needs and doesn't even begin to explain what is needed to help a child learn and grow. Parents are not prepared for all the difficulties that arise and they can only teach their children what they have learned from the environment in which they grew up in (family, family background, friends, community, media) and from their own lifetime of experience. All of these things combined create either a positive or a negative perspective about life which greatly impacts how we interact with others. This can be tragic because many people come from dysfunctional families and don't know how to care for themselves, let alone raise children and teach them how to become confident and responsible adults.

When my first daughter was born, I had absolutely no idea of how to raise a child. Basically, I was still a child myself and certainly not thinking responsibly as a mother should. My husband was not prepared for this task either, coming from another dysfunctional home. Thankfully, my firstborn was an easy child to care for and we spent many happy times playing together, reading stories and going to the park.

Just a few years later, my second daughter came along and I thought I was really prepared this time. Over four years of experience being a mom should count for something, right? Did I think I deserved a medal? Well, I found out quickly that every child is different. This one had colic and I didn't have a clue what to do. Fortunately, I had lots of family support during these and other difficult times.

As a grandmother, I can now look back to when I was raising my girls and see how my perspective on life caused me to make a lot of mistakes. Had I known then what I know now, I would have been a much better mother. Of course, I did really love my girls and tried my best to teach them right from wrong. Even though I messed up a lot, they did turn out to be intelligent, responsible and caring adults. They may be far from perfect and they struggle with their own issues, but I'm really proud of them both.

When my first grandson was born, I decided it was time to find out what it takes to be a good parent and I started doing a lot of research. Until then, I had never really thought about how much influence a parent had on their child's life. Their whole future depends mostly on what kind of environment they were raised in. A positive environment will help a child become confident and they will have strong self-esteem. A negative environment will destroy a child's confidence and they will have poor esteem. I began thinking about my own childhood and how much it had influenced me. Finally I understood why I had struggled with low esteem all my life. It was time to make some changes so I could positively influence my grown children, my new grandson and any future grandchildren.

The first thing I had to do was an honest evaluation of my life. It wasn't easy facing who I really was and I discovered that I had created a lot of my own problems. I tended to blame others for my unhappiness when I should have taken responsibility for my own actions. Feeling sorry for myself and allowing negativity to rule my life, was causing problems for myself and everyone around me. I didn't realize that I could control what I thought and did by changing my negative thoughts and self-talk into positive thoughts and self-talk. It isn't easy, but it can be done if we actively work on it all the time. We are definitely our own worst enemies, but with some hard work, we can actually become our own best friends.

People are creatures of habit. They get stuck doing the same things and even if they are aware that something is wrong, they don't always know what to do. Most parents tend to make the same mistakes as their parents did without even realizing what they are doing. Poor parenting habits can continue for generations unless changes are made. I realized that I was stuck myself in poor parenting habits and it made me both sad and happy. I was sad that I couldn't go back and fix the messes that I made, but I was also happy that it wasn't too late to change and become a better mother and an even better grandmother. It doesn't matter what we have done in the past or how old we are, we can always try to make amends for anything we have done and we owe it to our children to try.

My parents were probably unaware that they were having a negative effect on me. They provided for all my basic needs and brought me up in the Christian faith which taught me right from wrong. Their parenting skills were based on what they had learned from their parents, which included strict discipline but was lacking in the proper emotional support needed to help build confidence and esteem. This was not because they didn't love me, but because they didn't know how to do any better.

Over the centuries, parenting has changed. In ancient times, children were not considered to be important. They were owned by their parents who could discipline them in any way they wished, even to the point of selling them or killing them if they were unwanted. Can you imagine killing your own children if they were causing problems? How horrible is that? Children were raised to fear their parents and to be obedient if they wished a roof over their head and food to eat. Strict and often horrible punishments were given if the child did not obey their parents. These methods of raising children have changed in many countries however there are still some parts of the world that use these harsh methods.

Today we are discovering better ways of raising children and are using positive parenting methods. Instead of creating fear in a child and trying to control them, it is much better to love them and allow them the freedom to make choices. It is also important to set boundaries and enforce them so they will learn discipline and respect. Love is the most important thing we can give our children and it will help them grow into responsible, caring adults.

Finding a perfect solution to parenting is impossible as each child is different. However in all my research and from my own personal experience, I've concluded that being a positive role model can have the biggest impact on a child's life. Parents (or caregivers) are usually the first teachers that children have and they can help their children develop a strong sense of worth. Children see and hear everything their parents say or do. Spoken words will either build up our children or tear them down. Actions will leave a good impression or influence them in a negative way.

It is so important that we become the best possible role model we can be and teach our children by example. This doesn't mean we should beat ourselves up trying to be perfect because that just isn't possible. We are human and we will make mistakes. However, if we are lacking in some way or doing something we know is wrong, we need to address our own issues and become the person that we want our children to be.

The purpose of writing this book is to share some of the things that I have learned through personal experience and also from lots of research on parenting. The information is not intended as professional advice because I'm just an ordinary mother and grandmother who cares deeply about how children are being raised today. I have seen and felt what negative parenting can do to a child. Please use my insights as a guideline and I pray that you will be able to love and support your children in the best way possible.

CHAPTER ONE

CONFIDENCE AND SELF-ESTEEM

*Happiness and success are wrapped up in a package
called self-esteem.*

Did you know that confidence and self-esteem are not
actually the same thing? Many people use these words
interchangeably as I did until a few years ago, however
their meanings are slightly different. The dictionary can
be confusing so let me simplify for you. Confidence
describes how other people see you (from the outside)
and self-esteem describes how you see yourself (from
the inside).

Let's take a closer look at confidence which can be seen from the outside. Many people can have confidence in their abilities and are able to show this clearly to other people. If I am able to play the piano well or paint some beautiful pictures, I will be able to show this to other people and they will be able to see my confidence.

Now let's look at self-esteem which comes from the inside. Self-esteem is a term used in psychology to show an appraisal of a person's worth and value. It is a collection of beliefs and is how we see ourselves and how we feel about ourselves. When you look in a mirror, what do you see? If you like yourself and accept who you are, then you will have good esteem which will shine from the inside to the outside.

Why is it so important to have strong esteem? It helps you face life's difficulties with confidence and gives you the ability to make good choices. It helps you form good relationships and be an effective communicator. It allows you to live with purpose and reach your goals.

In order to have good esteem and a healthy self-concept, children need to feel love and encouragement from parents and peers. Children who have confidence and strong esteem:

- know their strengths and weaknesses
- can deal effectively with challenges
- enjoy interacting with others
- are optimistic and use positive self-talk

These are the children who grow up to be secure adults, being able to face their fears and deal effectively with everyday life situations.

On the other hand, children who lack confidence and have low esteem:

- are critical and disappointed in themselves
- get frustrated and give up easily
- become withdrawn
- don't want to try new things
- are pessimistic and use negative self-talk

These are the children who grow up to be adults with insecurities, fears and have difficulty dealing with everyday life situations.

In order to find happiness and success in life, it is critical to have both confidence and strong esteem. Some people have confidence in their abilities, but don't like something about themselves, so they have low self-esteem. You can have confidence and not have good esteem, but you can't have good esteem without being confident.

The good news is, esteem is not something we are born with; it is something we can learn at any point in our lives. Therefore, if you don't have good esteem now, you can start building it today. Once you have developed a strong esteem, then you will be able to help your children and others to build their esteem.

Here are some ways to help get you started on building esteem:

- Focus on your unique strengths and abilities. Everybody is different and that is okay.

- Stop comparing yourself to others. You DO NOT have to be like somebody else. You are great just the way you are.
- Change negative thoughts into positive thoughts. *"I can't do this" becomes "I can do this". "I am worthless" becomes "I am worthy". "I hate my job" becomes "I have a job and I am thankful to be working".*
- Learn to love yourself (not in a conceited way) and love others.
- Say positive affirmations daily. *"I like myself. I do a good job. I am a loving parent".*
- Avoid negative people, places and things when possible. They will just make you feel bad.
- Surround yourself with positive people who will encourage and uplift you.
- Read books, listen to CD's and watch DVD's on building esteem. Pass on what you have learned to family and friends.
- Don't listen to any bad things that others say to you. Try to feel good about the great person that you are.
- Don't try to be perfect. Nobody is perfect and you will just frustrate yourself trying to do the impossible. Just do the best you can in every situation.
- Allow yourself to make mistakes. The most successful people in the world have made lots of mistakes and this is how we learn and grow.
- Be thankful for what you have. Accumulating lots of stuff does not make you happy. Happiness comes from within.

CHAPTER TWO

BE A POSITIVE ROLE MODEL
Be the person you want your child to be.

Children learn by what they see and hear. They see how you treat them and also how you treat other people. They listen to how you speak to them and also how you speak to other people. This forms their idea of what life is like. If you are passing on positive messages to your children, they will develop a positive self-concept. If you are passing on negative messages to your children, they will develop a negative self-concept.

It is the responsibility of every adult to be a positive role model so their children will learn how to be a responsible adult who can influence others in a positive way.

As my own children grew, I did not realize the effect my words and actions would have on their future life. I was too busy trying to be the perfect wife, mother, housekeeper, cook, pet sitter, friend, teacher, chauffeur, volunteer and full time worker. My life revolved around myself and my insecurities. Looking back now, I can see that there were times I was a good role model but there were many more times when I was a poor role model.

Let's look first at the times when I believe that I was a good role model. Our family did spend many happy times together on festive occasions such as Christmas, Easter, Thanksgiving, birthdays and anniversaries. Daily meals were enjoyed together after which we watched quality TV programs like *Little House on the Prairie* and the *Waltons*. This was definitely a huge difference from the questionable programs that children watch today. We went camping, visited relatives and took family vacations to places like Nova Scotia and Disney World. Pictures were taken and put into photo albums to share for years to come. During these times our children learned the value of spending time together with family and friends and we can all look back at happy memories.

Now let's look at the times when I believe that I was not a good role model. Every family has problems and if anyone tells you they don't, they are trying to hide something. Our family had many times of turmoil between husband and wife, mother and daughter, father and daughter. There were misunderstandings, arguments, silences, criticisms, complaints and a basic lack of communication. Nobody knew the right thing to do because we hadn't been taught! All the dysfunction of generations past came marching in to tear apart and destroy. A lot of unhappy memories were created during these difficult times.

Children need to realize that their parents are not perfect people but they also need a good example to follow. My parents hid their problems and imperfections from me and this just sent out unrealistic messages to me. I thought there was something wrong with me because I was always getting into trouble and I was continually being told I was bad. My life was spent trying to become the perfect child that I thought my parents expected me to be and of course, I was never able to accomplish this.

Parents should let their children see them as real people so they will not try to live up to standards they can never reach. Let them know that you make mistakes just like everyone else in the world does. There is nothing wrong with showing your children that you are human because it will help them see life in a more realistic way. Share your special childhood memories with them and also talk about some of the difficult times (unless they are traumatic). Share your feelings and try to build a close relationship.

Are you the type of person that you would like your child to be?
   *Think about the way you dress. Do you look tidy or sloppy?

*Think about the way you talk. Do you speak nicely or do you swear, use inappropriate language or rude hand gestures?

*Think about the way you act. Do you treat other people with kindness and respect or do you show anger and violence?

*Think about your attitude. Is it positive or negative?

*Think about the way you care for yourself. Do you eat healthy food and exercise or do you eat junk food and sit watching a lot of TV?

*Think about the TV shows and movies you watch. Do you watch family programs and movies or ones that show violence, sex or use bad language?

*Think about your habits. Do you participate in positive, healthy activities or do you smoke, drink, use illegal drugs or view pornography?

Your children are watching you all the time and they will likely imitate you in many ways. Is there anything you should change about yourself, so you can be a positive role model? If you want to teach your children good habits, you need to show them good habits.

*If you want your children to be loving, than you must be loving.

*If you want your children to show respect, than you must show respect.

*If you want your children to show kindness, than you must show kindness.

*If you want your children to have integrity, than you must have integrity.

*If you want your children to be patient, than you must be patient.

*If you want your children to be forgiving, than you must be forgiving.

*If you want your children to have faith, than you must have faith.

*If you want your children to be positive, than you must be positive.

It's really simple but hard to do. You must be the person you want your child to be.

CHAPTER THREE

TEACH LOVE
Home should be a place where you feel safe and secure.

A home is a place where people live, eat and sleep. But a home should also be a place where love is felt, a place where families and friends gather to create special memories. It should be a place where you can feel safe and secure, a place where you can have fun.

When children live in a home with a warm, loving atmosphere, they will feel safe and secure, and it will be natural for them to love others easily.

I really love my children and always tried to do the best I could for them, but my love was not really the right kind of love. Children need unconditional love which gives them security and esteem. The love I gave my children was conditional love because that is the type of love that I received growing up. If I was good, I was loved. If I achieved awards, I was loved. If I did what I was told, I was loved. However, when I was bad, which was often, I was punished and sent off to my room. There I felt sad and alone, thinking that when I was bad, I was unlovable and had no value. So I tried to figure out what good things I could do to regain some love.

Is your love based on any conditions? It shouldn't be. Your love for your children and all family members should be unconditional, no matter what they do. If you have been raised in a negative or unloving environment, it can make it very hard for you to give love to your child. Since you can't give away what you don't have, you will need to work very hard at creating a loving home environment for your family.

We all need to be positive role models in our home and show love to everyone around us. Not just our children but everyone who comes into the home. This includes our family, friends and visitors. Showing our love will create a warm, comfortable atmosphere where everyone will feel safe and secure.

Don't just assume that your children know you love them. People DO NOT just know that you love them, you have to show them. Children have different personalities and require different levels of love. Some need lots of attention and others are okay with an occasional hug or positive comment. My two daughters were good examples of how different children can be. Determine what works best for your children but make sure you show love in some way. Give them a hug, a kiss on the cheek, touch their shoulder, hold their face in your hands and tell them you love them. Tell them how special they are, how happy you are to be their parents and how important they are to your family. Write a note, send a card, draw a picture.....there are so many little things you can do to show your love. I've heard many stories about people who have never heard their parents say they love them and this is so sad and unnecessary. It doesn't matter if you have never heard anyone say they love you, start by telling your children and make both of your lives better.

Parents need to be an example of love and teach their children to love others. This world is so full of hate and violence and it is often because people have not received enough love. We need to be a good example to others and show love to everyone we meet. Without love, our children will not be able to love themselves and others. Remember, you can't give away something that you don't have.

Fill your children with love every day so they will become confident and their esteem will grow. Love will help them deal with difficult situations in a positive way. Love will give their lives purpose and value. Love will help them become responsible adults.

Always make sure your children know that they are safe in their own home, that the door will be open to them even after they leave home to go to college, move into their own place or get married. Let them know that they can come home even if they have made a mistake and that you will help them no matter what. It is so important that you create a safe home environment where your children feel love. If they grow up feeling this love and security, they will be able to pass it on to their children and grandchildren.

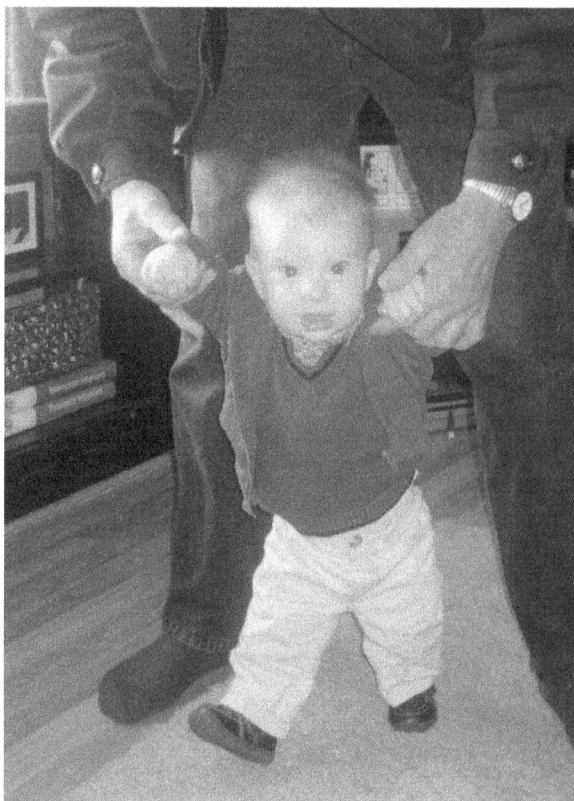

CHAPTER FOUR

TEACH ENCOURAGEMENT
and BE SUPPORTIVE
Encouragement helps build confidence.

When children are very young, they start learning the concept of success. I remember watching my girls when they started to roll over. They didn't do it right the first time, or the second, or third, but they kept trying until they succeeded and then they smiled because they felt good about themselves. It wasn't necessary for me to physically do anything to help them roll over, but it was important that I encouraged them so they would feel my support.

When children live in a home where they are encouraged and supported, it will build confidence and they will be able to encourage and support others.

Nurture your children and help them to develop their unique gifts and talents. All children have dreams and they imagine doing all sorts of wonderful things when they grow up. Children will tell you that they want to be a doctor, firefighter, artist, dancer, teacher, astronaut, and so on. Often, these dreams are pushed aside and forgotten because nobody takes the time to encourage them and support their ideas. Parents should help their children develop their skills and encourage them to follow their dreams. If these dreams are totally unrealistic or impossible, don't discourage them; just gently try to guide them towards other similar interests.

My girls didn't know exactly what they wanted to do after finishing high school, so I gave them time to figure it out, instead of pushing them to go to college as my parents had done. They both worked for a while and then decided on a career path which I totally supported. When they encountered difficulties or had trouble finding a job, I kept encouraging them to keep going until they were both successful. As for the college course that I took, it was a total waste of time and money and I never followed that path in my life.

Encourage your children to make their own choices (age-appropriate), so they can become independent. They won't always make good choices and you may not always agree with them, but try to be supportive, acknowledge their feelings and show respect. It is sometimes easier to make choices for your children, especially if you think they are wrong, but if you don't allow them to make their own choices and learn from the consequences, they will become dependent on you and not know how to make decisions in life, good or bad. Making choices for your children tells them that they are too stupid to make their own and that they need someone else to think for them.

When you allow your children to make choices, you still need to maintain control of these choices while you are teaching them the importance of making good and bad decisions. Young children need a lot of guidance, but you can still allow them to make some simple choices.
"Do you want cereal or toast for breakfast?"
"Would you rather wear your blue sweater or yellow sweater?"
"Do you want to go to the park or the petting zoo?"

As they get older, broaden the guidelines for their choices.
"I'd like to take you out for lunch. Would you rather go to (name 3 or 4 restaurants)?"
"Would you rather buy this one sweater for $100 or go to the discount store and get more items?"
"Other than black, what colour would you like your room painted?"

Family meetings are a good idea for making family decisions and learning how to encourage and support each other. Everyone participates and works together as a team to find solutions. Ask questions so it makes them think about whether their choices are good or bad.

"Will this work for you?"
"Is this what you really want?"
"Is there something else that might work better?"
"What problems might you encounter?"
"How can we help?"

When families work together and support each other, it creates a powerful bond that empowers the members to withstand any outside negative forces, such as peer pressure.

If you want your children to make good choices in life, it is important that they are well informed about various topics, especially the tough ones like smoking, alcohol, drugs and sex. Remember that your children learn from your own actions and lifestyle, so it is important that you set a good example. If you are abusing substances yourself or living a questionable lifestyle, it is telling your children that those behaviours are acceptable and they will be more likely to become an abuser themselves.

It is important that parents talk to their children about how certain substances can hurt people in a physical, emotional, mental or spiritual way. Make sure you are knowledgeable and keep up-to-date on all new information. Teach your children that it is okay to say no if anyone tries to pressure them into taking drugs, drinking, smoking or doing anything they know is not right. Encourage them to talk to you if they ever have any questions or problems. Peer support can be very hard to resist if your children do not have good esteem, so keep supporting them even when they do make poor choices.

When children are encouraged and supported, it helps them understand that their life has value and they will be able to encourage and support other people.

CHAPTER FIVE

TEACH EFFECTIVE COMMUNICATION
Effective communication is important for building good relationships.

Communication is difficult for all of us and if we don't communicate effectively, it will cause all sorts of misunderstandings and conflict.

When children live in a home where there is good communication, they will build good relationships with their family and other people.

Many parents do not know how to communicate well and are unable to teach their children. This creates all sorts of problems in the home and results in communication breakdown. My parents were raised in strict homes believing that children should be seen and not heard. They raised me the same way, expecting me to do what I was told and not question them. This was their way of teaching me to follow rules and respect authority. Unfortunately, it had a negative effect on me and I developed a fear of people. I was afraid of being laughed at. I feared making mistakes and being a failure. I felt unimportant and developed a low opinion of myself.

Children want to feel that their parents care about what they are saying. They want to feel like their ideas and words have value. Listening to your children is extremely important as it will keep the lines of communication open between you. I didn't always listen to what my children were saying because I was always too busy telling them what to do. By following the example I had learned, it had a negative effect on the relationship with my children.

If you want your children to keep talking to you as they get older, you have to build a close relationship with them. Talk about their interests, their friends, how they are doing in school. Talk openly about personal stuff like sex, drugs, alcohol, smoking, their eating habits. Make sure they have all the right facts about these topics. Ask lots of questions without prying too much. Ask them where they like to go, what they like to do, what kind of job they are interested in. Don't try to judge or criticize or be shocked, as this will turn them away from you. Don't control the conversation and give them your opinion. You may not agree with everything they say, but just listen and learn as much as you can about their life. What they think may not be important to you, but it may be very important to your children. Get involved and show an interest in everything they do. If you are a good listener, they will tell you lots.

A great way to build a relationship with your children is spending time with them one-on-one. Take them out shopping or visit their favourite restaurant just so you can chat and catch up. Take them on a short trip, maybe to the beach or on a weekend campout. This special time just for the two of you shows that you care deeply about them.

Talk to children in a positive, loving way and talk WITH them, not TO them. Use words that encourage and teach them valuable life lessons. When I was a child, I remember hearing my parents say little statements that were supposed to teach me something about life. They are called *Dadisms* or *Momisms* and are similar to quotes. You might have heard some of the more familiar ones:

> *Stop crying or I'll give you a reason to cry!
> *Am I talking to a brick wall?
> *You have things so easy...I remember when I was your age...
> *I taught you everything you know and you still don't know nothing.
> *A little pain never hurt anyone.
> *Do as I say, not what I do.
> *I'll tell you why. Because I said so, that's why.

Wow, what ridiculous statements to say to a child! There is absolutely no love expressed. No esteem building at all. Try very hard to communicate with your children even if they aren't talking much and don't seem to be listening to you. As children get older, they are struggling to find their independence and will try to separate from any parental control. It is easy just to give up and not bother trying to communicate with them, but this won't resolve anything. Keep in mind that children want to communicate with somebody. If they are not talking to their parents, they are probably talking to someone else who may be influencing them in a negative way.

CHAPTER SIX

TEACH THE VALUE OF TIME
Time spells love.

Children want to spend time with their parents because they naturally crave attention. Spending time together helps develop good relationships which is very important for families. The time and effort it takes to build a good relationship is well worth it.

When children live in a home where time is given to them, they will feel love and will want to spend valuable time with their own children.

Small children love bedtime stories. They crawl up on your lap or snuggle beside you and the warmth of their love is amazing. When my girls were small, I held them close to me and read stories of animals, princesses and cartoon characters. Reading is powerful. It helps children learn and stimulates their imagination. It also creates a close bond between parent and child. Experts recommend that parents help their children develop a love for reading because they will do better in school and show more creativity.

As your children grow, spend time doing other fun activities. Play games with them. Children love to play games; it teaches them how to be competitive and helps them build esteem.

There are many different types of games you can play according to their age. Young children like to play hide and seek or tag. Throwing a bean bag in a container or pin the tail on the donkey are also fun games. As they get older, introduce some board games, card games or word games and puzzles. Keep them simple and fun. Some children are very good at playing games and will win a lot. If they don't, make sure you allow them to win once in a while so they don't get discouraged and feel like a loser. Emphasize competition rather than winning and be a good sport when you lose in order to set a positive example. Tell your children that nobody can win all the time and there is no shame in losing. When they do lose, give them credit for trying and encourage them to play again.

Some other fun activities that you could enjoy with your children are:

- cooking or baking - make a grilled cheese sandwich or bake some yummy cookies
- watch a funny movie and laugh lots
- pack a picnic lunch and go to the park
- paint pictures or colour characters
- build a Lego town or blocks
- plant a garden
- create a puppet show
- go to an ice cream parlour
- put up a tent in your backyard and have a daytime campout

When your children are small, get them to help you with some simple chores. Taking time to help them clean up their toys, pick up their clothing and set the table will teach them responsibility. Make sure you tell them how important they are to the family by helping with the chores.

Get your children to participate in positive activities and support them by going with them. Both of my girls were involved in Girl Guides, so I participated as a leader. It was time consuming, but I enjoyed it thoroughly. There were some special moments spent together around the campfire and sharing in the daily events. I also taught my girls to play some simple pieces on the piano and took them to horseback riding lessons with me. These were times when I was being a positive role model and my children were learning some valuable life lessons.

Taking time to do things together as a family will help children feel like they belong and this is what we all want

- to belong. We do the craziest things just to belong to something or someone. We will wear clothing we don't like, listen to weird music, get tattoos, colour our hair red, or even risk becoming addicted to substances (tobacco, alcohol or drugs) just so we can belong. If your children feel like they belong to a loving, caring family who supports them, they are less likely to feel the need to try any inappropriate behaviours.

Spend as much time with your children as you can, so they will feel loved and wanted. Parents are often too busy to notice what their children are doing, but it is important that we take time to show them we are watching what they do and we care about them. Many parents allow their children to spend a lot of time alone, watching TV, playing video games and doing other activities that can result in a confused, angry, resentful or bitter adult. When I look back at the years when my children were growing up, I regret not spending more time with them. I missed out on so much and I wish I could go back and retrieve all those lost hours.

Parents often make promises to spend time with their children and then in their busyness, these promises are forgotten. Unfortunately this can have a negative effect on your children. They will feel that you forgot your promises because their life is not important and they will develop insecurities.

A good way to keep track of the time you want to spend with your children is to create a calendar and hang it where everyone can see it. Use a different colour pencil or marker for each child and mark down the dates that you are going to spend time with them. Mark down their birthdays, special events, park visits, play times and other dates that you want to remember. Being able to visually see their 'dates' marked on a calendar will make your children feel special and it will boost their esteem.

Keep in mind that as you grow older, you will want and need your children to be close to you. If you have spent happy times with them and developed a close relationship, your children will want to be there for you when you retire and move into a smaller home or retirement community.

Have you been too busy or tired when your children come to you and ask for time to play a game, read a story or help them with their homework?
If your children tell you that they want to talk to you, do you stop and listen or tell them to wait until later because you are on your way out?
Do you promise to take your children on a camping trip or to the zoo but keep putting it off because you can do it next year (which never comes)?

When you keep disappointing your children and ignoring their needs, you can almost guarantee they won't be there when you need them. Time is such a valuable commodity, so don't miss out on those special moments that could be wonderful memories.

CHAPTER SEVEN

TEACH THE VALUE OF DISCIPLINE
Discipline teaches responsibility

Discipline helps children learn appropriate behaviours, accountability and self-control. Society requires us to abide by laws and sets boundaries that give us security and protection. It is important that children learn how to follow rules and stay within boundaries that have been set and be aware of any consequences for their actions.

When children live in a home where fair rules and clear boundaries are made and enforced, they will become a responsible adult who understands the importance of proper discipline.

When your children are small, determine what the consequences will be for negative behaviours. Don't wait until they misbehave before you think about discipline. As soon as they can attend school, it is time to sit down with your children to discuss boundaries and determine consequences. Keep the rules age-appropriate and make changes when necessary by discussing them with the family. Keep the rules simple and easy to remember. Children should be able to memorize them and be able to repeat them back to you. Make sure they are fair, because children will not tolerate unfair rules.

A good way to avoid any confusion or misunderstanding is to create a chart explaining the rules and listing any consequences. Children will naturally try to get out of any punishments and they need to be reminded about what they have agreed to. When creating rules, try to phrase the words in a positive way by telling your children what you want them to do, not what you don't want them to do (there are certain exceptions).

On the next page is an idea of how you can create a rule chart. Each family is different, so use these ideas and adapt them according to age and number of children. Create one for the entire family or one for each child.

SAMPLE FAMILY RULES

- RESPECT YOURSELF AND EVERYONE IN THE HOUSE
- TALK POLITELY AND CALMLY
- TOYS PUT AWAY BY BEDTIME
- DINNER WILL BE EATEN TOGETHER DAILY
- COMPUTERS USED AS PER DAILY SCHEDULE
- PHONE CALLS UNTIL 10PM
- NO SWEARING or FIGHTING
- ALWAYS BEHAVE WHEN OUT IN PUBLIC
- NO DRINKING, SMOKING OR USING DRUGS
- NEVER GET INTO A VEHICLE WITH SOMEONE WHO HAS BEEN DRINKING OR USING DRUGS
- CURFEW IS 10 PM weekdays, 11 PM weekends

SAMPLE DISCIPLINE

- For disrespecting family, swearing, fighting, raising voice—time out followed by written and spoken apology
- For not putting away toys by bedtime—go to bed half hour earlier following night
- For misbehaving in public—quick time-out where suitable, lose a privilege (as determined)
- For not eating dinner with family (unless good reason)—clean up kitchen with no help
- For not following computer time schedule or making/receiving phone calls after 10pm—restricted use (as determined)
- For drinking, smoking or using drugs—grounding as appropriate, possible professional help depending on seriousness
- For getting into a vehicle with someone drinking or using drugs—grounding as appropriate, loss of privileges
- For missing curfew—take double time back from next curfew (if half hour late, take off hour)

Introduce your children to chores when they are young and try to make this a fun time for them. Play clean-up games and listen to music while the work is being done. Chores should never be given as a punishment and children should understand the importance of helping out around the house. Some chores can be done together as a family and this will help bond family members together. After the work is done, make sure everyone gets appreciation for doing a good job and remind them how valuable they are to the rest of the family. This would be a good time to have a special snack or do a fun activity.

When asking children to do something, be specific so they understand exactly what needs to be done and give them a time frame. *"Please go and pick up all the toys off the floor in your room now before supper and put them in your toybox".* Parents often assume that their children know what to do, but children aren't mind readers and they do forget. Reminding them can eliminate confusion and misunderstandings.

If your children are motivated to help, they will be willing to do what you ask. If your children do become stubborn and argue with you about doing chores, repeat your request calmly. If you control your emotions and don't get upset or angry, they will eventually just go and do what you ask. If they don't, it might be necessary to hold their allowance or not allow any privileges until the job is done. Every situation is different, so you will have to determine what the best solution is. Sometimes, it will seem like your child hates you, but when you enforce the rules, it helps them learn respect for leadership and they will be able to listen and respond in a positive way to their future teachers and bosses.

Never threaten to do something and then not follow through. You must always enforce the rules or your children won't understand where their boundaries are. All family members need to follow the same rules – parents, grandparents, siblings and anyone else who is in close contact, so the children will understand clearly what they need to do. If everyone follows a different set of rules, children will play family members against each other. When I misbehaved as a child, I would be spanked by my mother and sent to my room. Then I'd cry and get the attention of my dad who would feel sorry for me and sneak me treats, so I didn't really feel like I was being punished at all and I kept misbehaving.

When punishing children, make sure you separate the behaviour from the child and punish the behaviour, not the child. A child does something bad, the child itself is not bad. If a child breaks something, they have done a bad thing, but they are not bad. If you tell the child they are bad, this sends the message that there is something wrong with them and they will develop anxiety and insecurities.

Spanking is not the best type of discipline. It does not work if used a lot and only makes children think that violence is okay. As a child, I was spanked continuously and the only affect it had on me was to make me rebellious and tell me that hitting another person was acceptable. Sometimes a quick smack on the behind or a slap on the hand can be helpful in getting attention quickly when a small child is misbehaving, as long as pain is not inflicted.

Giving children a time out is a good way to discipline, especially if a child is out of control. This stops the misbehaviour and allows the child to calm down while reflecting on what they have done. Experts suggest that you give a child 1 minute time out for every year of their life. A 3 year old would get 3 minutes and a 10 year old would get 10 minutes. Longer time outs won't resolve anything and in fact might make the situation worse. Time outs should not be done in their bedroom or anywhere that they can be distracted by their stuff. Have a specific chair located where the child can sit comfortably and feel safe. Set a timer and tell your child they can get up when the timer goes off, ONLY if they have calmed down and are ready to talk to you. If they misbehave or yell during that time, add extra time as applicable to the timer. When the time is up, discuss the problem with your child and explain why their behaviour was not acceptable. Then tell them what will happen the next time they use this bad behaviour.

If a child misbehaves while you are out in public, don't let them think they can get away with misbehaving. Find somewhere that you can give them a shorter time out, like a bench in a mall or a park, or an empty chair in a restaurant or grocery store. They can even stand in a corner if need be, but children need consistency and follow-through so they know their parents are always in control of the situation.

When children show negative emotions they need to learn how to process them in a positive way and learn how to control them. Teach your children that it is okay to show emotions and that this is a normal part of life. However, children need to know they can't just react in any way they want to when they are feeling upset or angry. They need to understand that when we allow our emotions to control us, they can cause a lot of problems in life. When children see their parents controlling their own emotions, this is the best teacher of all. Try to stay calm even if you feel stressed by their actions and ask how they are feeling. Tell them to count to 10, loudly if they need to. Suggest that they jump up and down, hit a pillow, draw a picture or something that will take the focus off their anger. If they throw a temper tantrum, you may have to leave the room until they calm down, as long as they are not going to hurt themselves or do any damage. Then help them figure out what they should do, by remaining calm and talking through the problem.

Teach children to be responsible for their own actions. When something goes wrong in life, they shouldn't try to blame somebody or something else. If they are late for school because they woke up late, it is not the fault of the parent. If they didn't get their homework done because they were too lazy to do it, it isn't because the dog ate the paper. If they didn't get the job promotion because they didn't work hard enough, it isn't their co-worker's fault. I certainly did my share of blaming the weather, the traffic or somebody else for my failures and it gets to be a very bad habit that is often passed on to our children through our example.

Children need to learn that they must face the consequences of their actions. This helps them grow into a responsible adult. Make sure they understand why they are being punished, correct the behaviour and forget about it. Don't make a small matter into a big matter by reminding them about their misbehaviour. Once they have been disciplined, give them a hug to reassure them that you love them and move on.

Many kids today try to control their parents because they are confused about their boundaries. Some parents want to be friends with their children and allow their children to get away with everything. Parents need to parent and not be just a friend to their children. Children may hate you for punishing them, but it's more important what your child thinks of you 20 years from now than they do today. Just make sure you discipline them with love.

Other parents are too strict and this can have a negative impact on their children. Discipline needs to be fair and enforced so children will learn how to respect authority and rules. Children should not fear punishment, but should respect the authority of their parents. They need to know who is the boss in the home and it should never be the child.

Children will always try to push their boundaries as far as they can. This is part of their learning process and they need to explore life to the fullest. We shouldn't want our children to just follow every rule that they are given because some of them do need to be challenged. There will be times later in life when your children will need to question rules and try to figure out better ways to accomplish things in life.

Good leaders should always be reviewing rules and policies so they can replace anything that isn't working well with a way that is better. Discipline your children within the boundaries you have set but those boundaries do not have to be written in stone. Every child is different and you need to find out what works for the entire family. Review them and revise them when necessary.

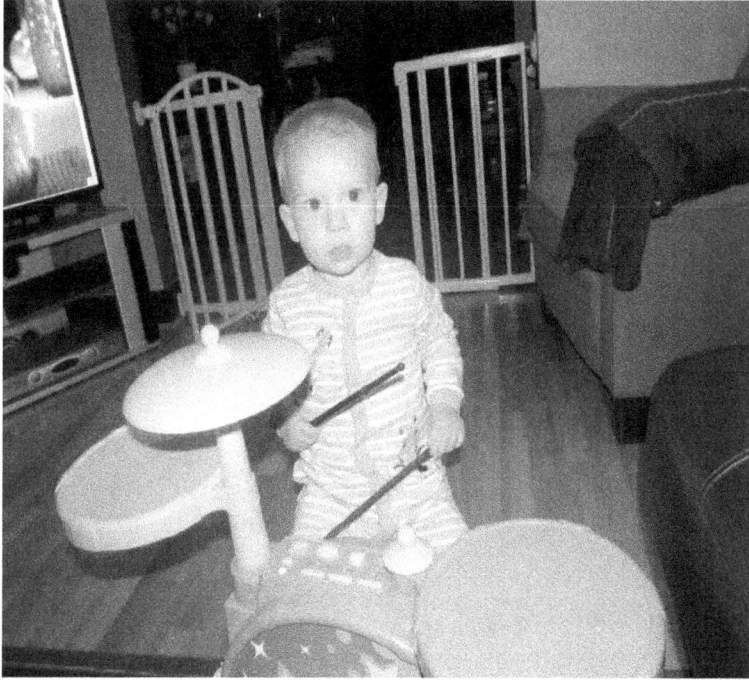

CHAPTER EIGHT

TEACH THE VALUE OF GOALS AND HOW TO ACCEPT FAILURE
Goals are the pathway to success.

Goals give purpose to life. Setting goals will help your children build confidence and increase their self-esteem.

When children live in a home where they set goals and learn to accept failure, they will be able to move ahead in life, learn from their mistakes and find success.

Until a few years ago, I hadn't really set any goals in life. I just did what I thought was expected of me and didn't celebrate too many successes. Now I realize how important it is to set goals and work diligently towards them. Goals are the way to find success in life.

Most parents want their children to be happy and successful in life. In order to accomplish this, you need to be actively working towards something. Setting goals will help you work towards whatever you are interested in achieving.

Setting goals is a good habit that can be started when children are small. Goals can be as simple as saving money for a special treat or a toy. As children get older, this can become a goal to join a team or go to a certain college.

Help your child write down their goals and keep working on reaching them. Break larger goals down in to smaller goals, so they don't seem so hard to manage. Find out what they are interested in and what they are good at doing. Get involved by working alongside them and help them keep track of their progress.

Children often learn that success is earned by doing something good or winning. Then when they fail, they become discouraged and disappointed. Some parents praise their children them when they do well in school or win at playing sports and this is fine as long as the child is not punished or put down when they fail.

Teach your children that life is not perfect and they will fail sometimes. Mistakes are a normal part of life, everyone makes mistakes, and it doesn't mean something is wrong with them. When children try something and fail, they need to be encouraged to keep going so they don't develop a fear of failure. This is one of the greatest fears people have and the one that can stop us from reaching our full potential in life. Children should learn that there is nothing wrong in making mistakes but that they can learn and grow from them. There are many famous people who failed lots of times before they became successful just because they kept pursuing their dream and didn't give up. Talk to them about some of the mistakes you have made in your life, but be careful you don't share anything that may be too overwhelming for them.

If your child doesn't do well on their report card, don't tell them they are stupid. If they don't make the team, don't tell them they aren't good enough. If they don't get that job, don't tell them they don't deserve it anyway. This will destroy their esteem and create insecurities. Instead tell them you are proud of them for trying their best and encourage them to do better next time. They need to know that you support them no matter what happens and this will help them become confident in their abilities. It will allow them to try new things and take risks in order to succeed.

When I was a child, I remember getting praise when I did something right but when I failed I don't remember any words of encouragement. I was expected to always do my best and if I didn't succeed, the results were ignored. Failure was devastating to me and I was always afraid to try anything new. As a mother, I tried very hard to encourage my children so they wouldn't have this terrible fear.

Would you rather hear, *"You're a failure and I'm disappointed in you"* or *"You tried your best and I'm proud of you"*? This should be an easy question to answer. However, when your children disappoint you, which one will you say? Saying the right thing is not easy because we are human, but parents do need to try very hard on using positive words with their children. Words can build up a child or tear them down and destroy their esteem.

Never tell your children that they should be ashamed of themselves for making mistakes as this will affect them negatively for a long, long time. Never tell your children that you knew they would fail and don't bring up past failures. Treat your children with respect and help them learn valuable lessons from their mistakes. Children need to learn how to accept failure, to learn from their mistakes and to keep going. Teach them never to give up easily.

CHAPTER NINE

TEACH ESTEEM
You aren't born with esteem, it is something you learn.

Esteem is a hard thing to build and easy thing to destroy. Developing good esteem is important so children will be confident in their abilities and not be influenced by worldly ideas.

When children are taught esteem, they will be confident in their abilities and be able to accept who they are.

In today's world, young people have huge issues about beauty and body image. Did you know that about 2/3 of all females avoid participating in some activities because they feel bad about how they look and almost half of all males are unhappy with their bodies? There is so much pressure on young girls and boys to be physically perfect and this creates all sorts of problems; stress, anxiety, depression, addictions, eating disorders and even suicidal thoughts.

All you have to do is read a magazine, turn on the TV or look at a computer to see images of **beautiful** people living **perfect** lives. These unrealistic images of beauty become reality, especially for our children and they can become obsessed their looks, losing all sense of their own unique identity.

Body weight has become a major issue and stats show that about 80% of girls have dieted by the time they are 18. This sounds extreme, but what really astounded me is that about 40% of girls have dieted by the time they are only 9! What are we doing to our young people today? Obviously, many children and teens are convinced that they are overweight and need to be on a diet. This is largely the fault of the media, but it can also be due to low esteem and living in an environment that doesn't promote healthy living.

Unfortunately many parents lack confidence themselves and have never developed a good self-concept so they don't know how to be a good role model. Many parents are dieting themselves and critical of their own looks. This will have a negative effect on their children and they will develop an unhealthy idea of beauty and body image. My own daughters had a poor role model because I was constantly obsessing about my looks and would never go out the door unless my clothing matched perfectly and every hair was in place. Every time I looked in a mirror, I would complain about my flaws and imperfections. I tried several diets and had poor eating habits. It's no wonder my girls developed a poor self-image and still worry about how they look today.

Parents need to help their children build esteem right from the beginning of their life so they will be able to withstand a certain amount of peer pressure and be able to make better choices. As children grow older, body image can often become the main focus of their lives and they will have a great need to be accepted by their peers. Without strong esteem, children can easily become influenced by negative peer pressure which can destroy their lives.

Discuss with your children how society creates unrealistic images of beauty that make us feel like there is something wrong with us. We are led to believe that we are too small or too big, too fat or too thin, too dark or too pale, too tall or too short. The world looks at us through a magnifying glass and shows us all our imperfections and flaws. If we wear the right clothing, have perfect skin, beautiful hair and a slim body we will be loved by everyone. WRONG! If we buy certain products, they will make us healthier, happier and successful. WRONG AGAIN! Surrounding ourselves with possessions can bring temporary happiness but it doesn't last and then we experience frustration and failure.

Children need to develop confidence in themselves and feel comfortable with how they look. Teach your children that it's okay to be different than other people and it's okay not to be perfect. We are all supposed to be different and we have special qualities that make us unique individuals.

Take your children to a crowded place like a mall or park and teach them to **people watch**. If you have never heard of **people watching**, it is a good way to observe how people look, dress, walk and talk without being intrusive. Sit quietly, glance around, don't focus on anyone for too long and nobody will even know you are watching them. This is an excellent way to build an awareness of people and give us a greater understanding of our differences. Discuss these differences with your children when you get home. Look around and see if you can find two people who look exactly the same. Of course, this would be hard and it is a good thing. Wouldn't it be boring if everyone looked the same! Now, see how many drop dead gorgeous women and amazingly handsome men you can find. You can always find some really nice looking people, but most of us are just average looking. We need to stop trying to compare ourselves to all those perfect images that we see and work hard at being the great and amazing person that we are meant to be.

What kind of expectations do we put on our children? Do we push them to be like others or do we teach them to bring out their own qualities and make them shine? Children need to have realistic expectations and not try to live up to the expectations of others.

Talk to your children about bullies. Help them understand that bullies want to hurt other people because they have been abused or bullied themselves and they don't know to be nice to people. Bullying others relieves their inner pain. Instead of being hurt by their actions, encourage your children to ignore the bullies and talk to you if they have any problems. Your children should understand that they are important and nobody has the right to hurt them physically, mentally or verbally.

Teach your children not to be afraid to stand up for what they believe in and not do something they know is wrong just to fit in or be accepted. Help them understand that it shows strength of character when they do the right thing even if it is hard. People who can withstand bullying and pressuring are often those who become great teachers and powerful leaders.

Some children become very dependent on using their computers, phones and other electronic devices. It is important that you monitor these things and pay close attention to what your children are doing without interfering too much with their independence. Restrict their use according to their age and how well they manage themselves. Too much use can cause them to become too dependent on them and create issues with their esteem.

CHAPTER TEN

PLANTING POSITIVE SEEDS
Children are a gift from God

Children are our greatest asset and they should be treated with love and respect. They are the future of our world and we need to raise them to be responsible, caring individuals.

If we plant positive seeds in our children, they will have fruitful lives and be able to pass on their knowledge and experience to their children and future generations.

Life is short and certainly not easy. Time passes by quickly and our children soon grow into adults. We need to spend time with our children and teach them what is important in life so they will have the skills needed to overcome difficulties and make good choices. Without a solid foundation, children will tumble and fall.

Children will automatically resist anything that will cause their lives to be uncomfortable, but they genuinely want to please their parents. We need to teach them how to become responsible and independent adults. Allow your children to experience life and face challenges. This is how they learn and grow.

Parents are normally the first and most important teachers that children have and we need to teach our children good, solid values so they can become great parents. Teach your children right from wrong. Teach them how to be positive. In today's world, children are being heavily influenced to develop and accept unethical behaviours. Many children are self-centered and lack respect for themselves and others. Parenting is becoming harder all the time but if children receive proper guidance, they are more likely to be successful in life.

Parenting is a full time job that requires a lot of time and effort. You can't be a part-time parent if you want a full-time child and a full-time family. Parents need to be actively involved in the lives of their children and show them unconditional love. Teach your children to:

   ✓love themselves and others
   ✓be a positive role model
   ✓have good manners

- ✓ be encouraging and supportive
- ✓ communicate effectively
- ✓ spend valuable time with their family and friends
- ✓ set and work towards realistic goals
- ✓ accept failure and learn from their mistakes
- ✓ become a responsible, caring adult
- ✓ be thankful for what they have
- ✓ help others and show kindness
- ✓ never give up

If you have issues of your own to change, then work on changing them first so you can provide your children with a good example. Remember that parents will have the biggest influence on their children. Think of a family as a team playing **Follow the Leader**. Parents are the leaders and the children are just following what is happening in front of them. Make sure you are influencing them in a positive way. Teach them basic values and help them build esteem. If your children feel good about themselves they will have a much better chance to survive in a world that promotes hatred, violence, greed and selfishness.

You will make mistakes because you are human. It is not possible to be a perfect parent and if you try to achieve perfection, this will send negative messages to your children. Making mistakes is part of life and children have to learn how to deal with them in a positive way. Don't beat yourself up when you make mistakes. Just be real and keep trying to be the best imperfect parent you can be.

We sometimes try to protect our children from things that will help them become a strong individual. They need to face difficulties, failures and mistakes. They need to understand that life will not always be easy or fair, but that you will always be there to support them and that you love them unconditionally.

There are many good books that provide detailed information on how to effectively raise children. It would be impossible to follow all of their advice, however it can be helpful to compare ideas since every child is different. The most important thing to remember is that all children are special and they need your love more than anything else.

CONCLUSION

It is the responsibility of every adult to be a positive role model so their children will learn how to become a responsible adult who can influence others in a positive way.

When children live in a home with a warm, loving atmosphere, they will feel safe and secure, and it will be natural for them to love others easily.

When children live in a home where they are encouraged and supported, it will build confidence and they will be able to encourage and support others.

When children live in a home where there is good communication, they will build good relationships with their family and others.

When children live in a home where time is given to them, they will feel love and will want to spend valuable time with their own children.

When children live in a home where fair rules and clear boundaries are made and enforced, they will become a responsible adult who understands the importance of proper discipline.

When children live in a home where they set goals and learn to accept failure, they will be able to move ahead in life, learn from their mistakes and find success.

When children are taught esteem, they will be
confident in their abilities and be able to accept who
they are.

If we plant positive seeds in our children, they will
have fruitful lives and be able to pass on their
knowledge and experience to their children and
future generations.

HAPPY PARENTING!

ABOUT THE AUTHOR

Brenda Silveira, the Author of *The Caterpillar to Butterfly Self-esteem workbook,* is known for inspiring people while building their self-esteem through her workshops, blogging and Confidence Coaching.

Her latest title, *Grandma's Notes on Parenting,* gives empowerment to new parents by highlighting a few simple ways to raise children in a positive environment. Brenda's candid recollection of her own lifetime of struggles helps individuals to realize they are not alone.

Brenda, a graduate of Stratford Teacher's College, a Girl Guide leader, Guide Commissioner and former owner of a housekeeping and yard maintenance company, is also the creator of *I M Confident Niagara Canada*, a project that promotes esteem building through a website that has information and visual presentations.

Be inspired by Brenda's writing by visiting her website at www.imconfident.com .